Matthew Sleeth, MD

Blessed Earth

Part 1
Guidebook

Hope for Creation

ZONDERVAN® Dot&Cross.
www.andcross.com

ZONDERVAN.com/
AUTHORTRACKER
follow your favorite authors

ZONDERVAN

Hope for Creation Guidebook
Copyright © 2010 by Blessed Earth and Dot&Cross

Requests for information should be addressed to:
Zondervan, *Grand Rapids, Michigan* 49530

ISBN 978-0-310-32486-7

Written by Matthew Sleeth, Nancy Sleeth, and Michael Colletto.
Edited by Michael Colletto.
Produced by Dot&Cross and represented by Kevin Small of smallbooks.com
Cover and interior design: Seth Herman

Printed in the United States of America

10 11 12 13 14 15 16 /DCI/ 20 19 18 17 16 15 14 13 12 11 10 9 8 7 6 5 4 3 2 1

Dedication

To David Wenzel, with love and prayers, for making dreams come true.

Contents

How to Use This Guidebook

The *Blessed Earth* film series is designed to challenge God's people to think critically and biblically about the issue of creation care. Whether you are exploring this issue on your own or within a group at home, school, or church, don't feel like you have to read every section or answer every question in this guidebook. Take your time, set your own pace, and simply open your heart to God. Allow Him to use this material to a change your life.

For individuals:
If you have access to your own copy of the DVD and wish to explore the content in greater depth on your own, we recommend that you watch each film session first, then working through the corresponding chapter of this guidebook. If you have time, watch the film a second time to continue to flesh out your answers.

For groups:
If you're sharing a copy of the DVD and exploring the sessions in a group setting, we recommend that you read through each session chapter first in preparation for your group discussion.

Before the session: Read the chapter in advance. This guide was designed to be easy to understand, so you'll be able to answer many of the questions without having seen the films. Answer as many questions as you can (but don't feel like you have to answer them all). Fill out the Action Plan for today, this week, this month, and this year. If you'd rather, simply make a few notes as you read through—whatever helps you feel prepared to meet with your group.

During the session:
1. Watch the film together.
2. If the group is large (more than 10 people), divide into discussion groups of six or fewer. Discuss the session and share your answers and action plans. Do not feel like you must get to every question.
3. If you split up the group, bring everyone back together to share highlights from your discussions and share one or more goals with the whole group.
4. Assign the next chapter.

For group leaders:

You do not need to be a teacher or "expert" to lead a group—you just need a desire to share the call to care for creation. If you're interested in leading a group discussion, please visit blessedearth.org and download the free Leader's Guide for additional ideas and instructions.

Thank you for sharing this journey with us. We are grateful for all you are doing to care for God's creation!

—Matthew and Nancy Sleeth

Introduction

Most of us are familiar with the story of creation recorded in Genesis. In six days, God created all the elements of the world—light, water, land and vegetation, the heavens, animals, and, finally, man. When everything was complete, God stood back and sized up what He'd created … and He declared that it was good—very good.

Because God believes in the value of the world, we should too. Everything God created is worthy of being cared for and protected. In *Hope for Creation* we will explore how we can show our love for God and for our neighbors by caring for His creation. My personal journey began when I started examining the Bible in the context of God's creation, and it's changed me forever; I promise, if you let the Holy Spirit work in you, this journey will change your heart—and your life—too.

—Dr. Matthew Sleeth
Executive Director, Blessed Earth

Session 1
Light

Session Summary

❝ In the beginning, God created the heaven and earth, and the earth was without form and void; and darkness was upon the face of the deep. And the Spirit of God moved upon the face of the waters. And God said, 'Let there be light,' and there was light. ❞

—Genesis 1:1–3 (NIV)

This was the beginning of the beginning—the moment when God chose to create a universe for His own glory. God speaks the first sentence of a love story that will include all creatures and all people throughout all the ages ... and it all begins with light.

Everyone we know and everything we see starts with God speaking light into existence. Scripture is full of references to light: light is used to represent God's goodness (Psalm 56:13), a guide (Psalm 43:3), and the truth (John 3). God Himself is light (1 John 1:5). So, it's not surprising that when God sends His only begotten Son, He is called the "Light of the World" who conquers all darkness. And we, as followers of Jesus, are called to be children of light (Ephesians 5) and the light of the world (Matthew 5).

In choosing to follow Christ, we become new people with new priorities. God changes our hearts ... and our behaviors change, too. It's not about following a list of rules; it's about following the lifestyle of Jesus.

Just before Jesus left this earth, He said, "Go into the world and preach the gospel to all the creatures, baptizing them in the name of the Father, the Son, and the Holy Spirit and teaching them to obey everything I've commanded you." The very first commandment we were given in the Bible is recorded in Genesis 2:15. We were told to tend and care for this garden—the earth. We can't go out and make disciples while simultaneously destroying the water, the air, and the creatures that God loves. If we don't respect the world around us, we're missing a major part of what God commanded us to do.

It's time for the church, as children of the light, to take a leadership role in caring for the planet. And it will be good.

Reflections on Light

My first scientific encounter with light occurred in kindergarten. I can't recall my teacher's name, but I remember the experiment we conducted.

Our class filled two clay pots with dirt. We planted bean seeds in both pots and watered them. We then placed one pot in a closet and shut the door and put the other outside in a courtyard, in the sunshine.

After a number of days, both plants sent up shoots—and for a short while they resembled each other. Both grew on the energy stored within the planted seed. As the days passed, the plant in the sun began to change. It turned green and beautiful. The plant in the dark closet continued to grow for awhile, but it looked pale and spindly. It never produced any fruit or seeds of its own.

What I learned in kindergarten is that life runs on sunshine. Irrespective of whether it's you, me, or a tree, life on earth is dependent on the element of light.

When we give ourselves over to God, we step from darkness into a great light. The light is necessary for beauty, growth, and bearing fruit. We cannot supply the light on our own any more than the plant in the closet can make itself green.

—Dr. Matthew Sleeth

Session Notes: Light

As you watch the first film session on **Light**, feel free to use the following page to jot down any notes, thoughts, and questions.

Hope Begins with a Changed Heart

1
  ❝ *And God said, 'Let there be light,' and there was light. God saw that the light was good, and he separated the light from the darkness.* **❞**

—*Genesis 1:3–4 (NIV)*

Why do you think the creation story begins with light?

2
  ❝ *When we behold the light and brightness of the sun, the golden edges of an evening cloud, or the beauteous rainbow, we behold the adumbrations of His glory and goodness, and in the blue sky, of His mildness and gentleness.* **❞**

—*Jonathan Edwards (1703–1758), Reflections of God's Glory*

Can you recall an experience when light made you feel closer to God— through an inspiring sunrise, rainbow, light sheeting through the clouds, or sunset? Describe the scene and what it taught you about God.

Dr. Sleeth's wife, Nancy, asked him two questions that started him on his journey of spiritual and environmental discovery. It began with the question, "What's the biggest problem in the world today?" After some thought, Matthew answered, "The world is dying." In what sense is the world "dying"? Give examples.

3

4
Dr. Sleeth's wife followed up with a second question: "If the world is dying, what are you going to do about it?" Dr. Sleeth didn't have an immediate answer to the second question, in part because the problem seemed so overwhelming. What is your initial reaction when you learn about overwhelming problems?

Dr. Sleeth explains, "As the light of the world, Jesus is a beacon for all of us. He's a model of how to live, how to conduct our everyday life." In what sense is Jesus a model for our everyday choices?

5

6 *« Jesus asks us to become children of the light. »*

—*Dr. Matthew Sleeth*

What does it mean to become a "child of the light"? What actions are "light" and what actions are "dark" in terms of caring for creation?

7 A regular incandescent bulb wastes 90 percent of the energy it consumes producing heat instead of visible light. In what ways do we waste our energy and not produce the light that God wants us to?

❝ *By contrast, an energy-efficient bulb uses about 90 percent of the energy going in to make light. It's light that we can do something by.* **❞**

8

—*Dr. Matthew Sleeth*

In practical terms, how does stewarding our resources more wisely show our love for God and our neighbors around the world?

❝ *This light shines in the darkness, and the darkness can never extinguish it.* **❞**

9

—*John 1:5 (NLT)*

❝ *For the darkness is disappearing, and the true light is already shining.* **❞**

—*1 John 2:8 (NLT)*

In what ways do these descriptions of light offer us hope? In terms of caring for God's creation, what evidence do you see of "light already shining"?

A Changed Heart = A Changed Life

Caring for God's creation intersects with every aspect of our Christian walk, including how we steward electricity and light. If we can do 10 percent better each year, we are headed in the right direction!

Matthew has always been obsessed with light; our home has been the testing ground for lighting technology. We have tried every new kind of light bulb on the market, going back more than twenty years to those first energy-saving bulbs that buzzed and gave off a harsh light. When we moved the last time, a friend jokingly suggested that we start a Museum of Light Bulb History.

 Energy-saving light bulbs use about one-quarter the energy of standard light bulbs and last up to ten times longer.

If you have been reluctant to buy energy-saving light bulbs because you think they give off an unflattering light, give the new "soft" and "warm" bulbs a try. Their light is indistinguishable from regular light bulbs. Plus, the wide selection of bulbs available today makes it possible to find the right energy-saving bulb for every imaginable wattage and fixture. Several light bulb manufacturers even make CFLs designed for use in candelabras and on dimmer switches.

Energy-saving bulbs do cost more initially, but the average payback in energy savings takes less than a year—even sooner if you use rebates or find bulbs on sale. Conventional bulbs are the most energy-intensive, followed by halogens, then compact fluorescents. The most efficient bulbs are light-emitting diode (LED) bulbs.

Turning lights off when not in use is the easiest way to save energy. Dimming your lights also can cut back on electricity bills.

 About 90 percent of the electrical current used to power standard light bulbs creates heat instead of light.

This makes energy-saving bulbs not only vastly more efficient, but also much safer. According to an EPA Energy Star fact sheet, if every American home replaced just one standard light bulb with an energy-efficient bulb, we would save enough energy to light more than 3 million homes, retain more than $600 million in annual energy costs, and prevent offgassing equivalent to the emissions of more than 800,000 cars. Simply changing our light bulbs can also save lives that would otherwise be lost due to respiratory illnesses and asthma attacks caused by air pollution from coal-fired power plants, especially among children and senior citizens.

One common question about CFLs concerns the mercury they contain. It's true: a CFL bulb contains a minuscule amount of mercury (4 mg on average), about one-fifth of the mercury found in the average watch battery and less than 1/600th of the mercury found in a home thermostat. However, the amount they contain is small compared to the amount of mercury that coal-burning power plants emit to power the much-less-efficient incandescent bulb. A power plant will emit four times as much mercury to power a 60W incandescent bulb as compared to an equivalent CFL.

Those signs you see when you go fishing warning children and pregnant women to avoid eating the catch are not because of toxins dumped into the water. The concern over mercury poisoning comes primarily because of the mercury emitted from coal-fired power plants that settles in our rivers and lakes. To properly dispose of a burned-out CFL, just drop it off at a local Home Depot or IKEA store, or check out www.earth911.org for other safe disposal options.

The bottom line: using compact fluorescents cuts back on your electric bill, is safer for the environment, and better for people.

—*Nancy Sleeth*

Adapted with permission from *Go Green, Save Green: A Simple Guide to Saving Time, Money, and God's Green Earth* by Nancy Sleeth (Tyndale, 2009)

Good Steward Action Plan: Light

Instructions

1. Pick two or more new actions from the suggested lists to commit to today, this week, this month, and this year—or come up with your own ways to conserve light and electricity.
2. Go to blessedearth.org and join our community of Good Stewards. Explore the website to find additional ideas for saving energy and becoming a better steward of God's creation.
3. We will send encouragements to you, and help you stay on track. We're all in this together, so share your journey. Let us know what was easy, and what was difficult; inspire others with your story!

Today, Lord, help me to:

(pick at least two of the following goals, or come up with your own actions)

- Turn off lights when I leave the room.
- Rely on natural light as much as possible.
- Memorize at least one Scripture about light (see "Digging Deeper" section at the end of this chapter).
- Pray for the millions of people in the world who live without a reliable source of electricity.
- Pray for the millions of people in the world who exist in spiritual darkness.

1. _____

2. _____

This week, Lord, help me to:

**(pick at least two of the following goals, or
come up with your own actions)**

- At night, walk through my house with a flashlight and note how many lights are left on 24/7 (computers, audio equipment, etc). Eliminate as many as possible by plugging these appliances into power strips and turning them completely off when not in use.
- Switch at least seven incandescent bulbs to energy-efficient bulbs. (LED are best, then CFL, then halogen, then dimmable or lower wattage incandescent.)
- Encourage family and coworkers to turn off lights when they leave the room.
- Place at least one Scripture about light in a place that I see often (on the refrigerator, on my computer, next to an outlet or light switch).

1. _____

2. _____

_____

❝ *I love the symbolism of beginning our Genesis
2:15 journey by changing light bulbs.* **❞**

—*Dr. Matthew Sleeth*

This month, Lord, help me to:

**(pick at least two of the following goals, or
come up with your own actions)**

- Switch *all* incandescent bulbs in my home to energy-efficient bulbs.
- Use solar lighting outdoors.
- Install motion detectors outdoors and in the garage.
- Encourage my church or place of work to replace incandescent bulbs with LED bulbs in exit signs (which are on 24/7). The payoff for the initial investment is only a couple of months—after that, they will continue to save on electricity bills for years to come.
- When rooms are empty but lights are left on, turn them off—including conference room lights, TVs in public places, and restroom lights.

1. _____

2. _____

This year, Lord, help me to:

**(pick at least two of the following goals, or
come up with your own actions)**

- Look around the house at the all the items that emit light, and see if I can give some away to people who have less. How many clocks do I really need? Aquariums? TVs? Computers? Electronic pictures? Try to distinguish between wants and needs.
- Ask my church if I can post small signs beside every light switch, asking people to turn off the lights.
- Be a light unto my congregation: start a creation care column in the weekly bulletin, church newsletter, or on the church website.
- Share the light with my community: when people notice me turning off lights, explain that I am motivated by love for God and for my neighbors.
- Use some of the money I saved on my electricity bill this year to purchase CFL bulbs and donate them to my church or to low-income families. Share the light of Jesus: go door to door to distribute energy-efficient light bulbs.
- Electricity for light comes primarily from coal. Do some research on mountaintop removal on the Internet. If my heart is moved, show a film, such as *Mountain Mourning*, to my faith group, Sunday school class, or family. Discuss what we can do collectively to help save God's mountains.

1. _____

2. _____

Digging Deeper: *What Scripture Says About Light*

Light gives order to our lives. The rhythm of light and dark allows humankind to establish a daily time of activity, and a daily time of rest. God filled the world with light "to govern the day and night, and to separate the light from the darkness." *(Genesis 1:17)*

The seasons, established by the earth's rotation around the sun, further order our lives with times for planting, growing, harvesting, and feasting. By creating light, God gives us a way to "mark off the seasons, days, and years." *(Genesis 1:14)*

Light is also a symbol of God's goodness. When God gives light, it is "good" *(Genesis 1:19)* **When God removes light, as He did during the plagues upon Egypt, chaos ensues.** "During all that time the people could not see each other, and no one moved. But there was light as usual where the people of Israel lived." *(Exodus 10:23)*

When the Israelites are commanded to build the tabernacle, they are instructed to "keep the lamps burning continually" *(Exodus 27:20)* and to "set them so they reflect their light forward." *(Exodus 25:27)*

It is not surprising, therefore, that Isaiah describes the coming of the Messiah as a time of light: You will be "a light to the Gentiles, and you will bring my salvation to the ends of the earth." *(Isaiah 49:6)* "All nations will come to your light; mighty kings will come to see your radiance." *(Isaiah 60:3)*

Light is not only a symbol of God's goodness; it is the symbol of God's Son. "John himself was not the light; he was simply a witness to tell about the light. The one who is the true light, who gives light to everyone, was coming into the world."*(John 1:8–9)* "The Lamb is the light." *(Revelation 21:23–24)*

Jesus refers to Himself as the light: "I am the light of the world. If you follow me, you won't have to walk in darkness, because you will have the light that leads to life." *(John 8:12)* "I have come as a light to shine in this dark world, so that all who put their trust in me will no longer remain in the dark." *(John 12:46)* "My light will shine for you just a little longer. Walk in the light while you can, so the darkness will not overtake you.

Those who walk in the darkness cannot see where they are going." *(John 12:35)*

When Jesus is crucified, light is temporarily extinguished. "The light from the sun was gone. And suddenly, the curtain in the sanctuary of the Temple was torn down the middle." *(Luke 23:45)*

Yet these two millennia later, His light continues to shine. We are called to "to live as children of the light and the day." *(1 Thessalonians 5:5)* "For once you were full of darkness, but now you have light from the Lord. So live as people of light! For this light within you produces only what is good and right and true." *(Ephesians 5:7–9)*

God is the Creator of light, and His Son is the light and the one who shines within and through us. "For God, who said, 'Let there be light in the darkness,' has made this light shine in our hearts so we could know the glory of God that is seen in the face of Jesus Christ." *(2 Corinthians 4:6)*

One way we can live in the light is to be good stewards of God's creation; living in the light allows us to share the light of God the Creator and Jesus His Son. "You are the light of the world—like a city on a hilltop that cannot be hidden. No one lights a lamp and then puts it under a basket. Instead, a lamp is placed on a stand, where it gives light to everyone in the house. In the same way, let your light shine before men …" *(Matthew 5:14–16)*

The light of Jesus gives the environmental movement hope. "Jesus lived the truth of this commandment, and you also are living it. For the darkness is disappearing, and the true light is already shining." *(1 John 2:8)*

Adapted with permission from *The Gospel According to the Earth: Why the Good Book Is a Green Book* by Matthew Sleeth (HarperOne, 2010)

Session 2
Water

Session Summary

❝ *And God said, 'Let there be an expanse between the waters to separate water from water.' So God made the expanse and separated the water under the expanse from the water above it. And it was so.* **❞**

—Genesis 1:6–7 (NIV)

Water is an indispensable building block of life. Our very bodies consist mostly of water. Without water, life on this planet would not exist.

God was extravagant with water—He covered nearly two-thirds of the planet with it. Some people have described the earth as a "water planet."

But there's a problem: 97 percent of the water on earth is saltwater—the briny, ocean water we all remember tasting as a child on our first trip to the beach. And there's a second problem—about 85 percent of our fresh water is locked up in polar icecaps. This means that of all the water on earth, less than one half of 1 percent is drinkable and accessible to us. Fresh water is relatively rare!

Yet water is so much more than a physical necessity of life. It's a symbol that Christ uses over and over again to describe Himself. Water is God's symbol of rebirth, His metaphor for resurrection to a new life.

Jesus Himself was baptized in the water of the Jordan River as a symbol of what was to come, a physical death and a resurrection to eternal life.

Being a good steward means we must recognize the powerful role water plays in our lives, physically and spiritually.

Reflections on Water

I was meeting with a group of graduate students from around the world. In a relaxed moment, the students started talking about what they found most striking about American culture. They brought up the size of our grocery stores, our religious and ethnic tolerance, and our friendliness.

One woman explained that she was from a small farming village on the Korean peninsula. When she came to school in the U.S., it was her first time out of her rural setting. What is it like to live in rural Asia for decades and then suddenly be beamed up to urban America? "What strikes me as the most amazing thing," she said, "is that in America everyone empties their bladder in gallons of pure drinking water."

Her cheeks blushed, and she looked around the room to see what the reaction would be.

One flush of the average American toilet is more fresh drinking water than one third of the world uses in a day. As access to clean water becomes increasingly rare, followers of Christ must become better stewards of this precious gift.

—*Dr. Matthew Sleeth*

Session Notes: Water

As you watch the second film session on **Water**, feel free to use the following page to jot down any notes, thoughts, and questions.

Hope Begins with a Changed Heart

 ❝ *Say you fill a bathtub with about thirty gallons of water. Of that thirty gallons, one gallon would represent the fresh water on earth. And of that one gallon, one teaspoon would represent the amount that's drinkable and accessible. In other words, out of an entire bathtub, one teaspoon represents all the fresh water on earth that we can get to.* **❞**

—*Dr. Matthew Sleeth*

Although nearly two-thirds of the planet is covered in water, very little is drinkable and accessible. Why is fresh water precious? In what ways do we take it for granted?

 Dr. Sleeth says that "in addition to serving its utilitarian purpose, water can be a source of great joy." Recall a particularly significant time in your life involving water and describe how it made you feel.

Dr. Sleeth lists some examples of water being used in the Old Testament: "Moses hits a rock and water comes out. Jonah is propelled to Nineveh. God parts the Jordan for Joshua's army to go through and uses water to select Gideon's 300 warriors. The prophet Elisha uses water to cure Naaman's leprosy. Rebekah watering the camels at the well is a sure sign of her beautiful and kind heart."

Reflect on the significance of one of these (or another) Old Testament reference to water.

3

ff Water plays an equally important role in the New Testament. Jesus' first recorded miracle is to turn water into wine. He calms the sea when it's stormy and his disciples are in the boat. Jesus even walks on water to show His control over nature. ""

—*Dr. Matthew Sleeth*

4

Reflect on the significance of one of these (or another) New Testament reference to water.

5 When Jesus meets the Samaritan woman at the well, He tells her, "Everyone who drinks from this well will be thirsty again, but whoever drinks the water that I have, they will never thirst again." How can the "living waters" that Jesus offers help quench our thirst for material things?

6

❝ I try to appreciate water now. It's a gift rather than just an entitlement. For much of my life, I thought water was just something that came out of the hose or the sink. But it's so much more than that. All over the world, there are millions of people who have to walk miles just to get a single jug of water. They dig wells, they plant, and they simply have to pray for the rains to come. ❞

—*Dr. Matthew Sleeth*

Why do most of us say a prayer of thanks when we eat a meal, but not when we brush our teeth, turn on the shower, or wash our clothes? How can saying a prayer of thanks alter our stewardship habits?

A Changed Heart = A Changed Life

Last summer, we visited a friend on his family land in eastern Tennessee. After our picnic, I dipped a five-gallon bucket into the barrel that connects to a rainspout on the roof and started to carry water to their newly planted saplings. After the first round, I realized that five gallons was too heavy for me to carry any significant distance, so I started filling the bucket halfway full. Despite the drought, they had enough water collected in the makeshift rain barrel to bring several gallons to each young tree.

Driving home, I told Matthew that I had never really thought about how much water weighs and how much energy it must take to pump it up from the river and to our home. It takes about 3.5 gallons to flush a traditional (pre–1992) toilet, and about 1.6 gallons to flush a low-flow toilet. Imagine if we had to carry that water from several miles away, like the people Matthew met when practicing medicine in Honduras. I think I would be much more careful about the water I pour down the drain.

The Bible is full of references to women drawing water from wells—women like Rebekah, who was kind to God's creatures and remembered to water the camels, and the Samaritan woman with five husbands, who met Jesus and found eternal life. These women were reminded daily that water is a gift from God, not something to take for granted when we turn on the tap.

Carrying those pails of water to the saplings reminded me that it's not just water we conserve when we take shorter showers; it's also the energy it takes to transport that water. It requires loving and grateful hearts to appreciate the gifts right before us.

The average U.S. household consumes about twice as much water every day as the average home in Britain.

There are a lot of simple changes you can make to save water inside the home. For example, something as simple as turning off the faucet while brushing teeth and shaving can save a family of four about 48 gallons of water a day. Also:

Install low-flow showerheads. If you tried a low-flow showerhead years ago and were not satisfied—try again. They've improved dramatically.

Readily available at hardware and home improvement stores, low-flow showerheads can cost less than $10, and installation can be done by a homeowner.

Only run the dishwasher and clothes washer with full loads. We have an energy-efficient front-load washer, which not only saves electricity and water, but also spins out most of the moisture, so clothes dry much more quickly. Use the coldest water setting that gets the job done, and don't wash items such as pants, skirts, dresses, and sweaters every time you wear them—they'll last longer and you'll save time, water, and energy.

Fix leaky and inefficient toilets. Toilets are the biggest water users in the home. A leaky toilet can waste 200 gallons of water every day. Also, if you do not have an efficient toilet, try inserting a couple of bricks or 1-liter bottles filled with water in the toilet tank to reduce the amount of water wasted with each flush.

As much as 40 percent of our drinking water is flushed down toilets.

To reduce water waste outside in our lawns and gardens, one of the simplest things you can do is reclaim your water. By collecting water that has been used for bathing or other household duties and using it to water your plants, you can save up to 300 gallons per month. Or go one step further and install a rain barrel to collect water from your downspouts.

Also, use a spray nozzle on your garden hose to save up to 6.5 gallons per minute and, instead of using regular sprinklers, water your flowerbed and garden using drip irrigation or a soaker hose. This method saves water by minimizing evaporation and watering only the base of your plants. Similarly, mulching your plants reduces the amount of water lost through evaporation, limits weed growth, and improves soil conditions.

—Nancy Sleeth

Adapted with permission from *Go Green, Save Green: A Simple Guide to Saving Time, Money, and God's Green Earth* (Tyndale, 2009)

Good Steward Action Plan: Water

Instructions

1. Pick two or more new actions from the suggested lists to commit to today, this week, this month, and this year—or come up with your own way to be a better steward of water.

2. Go to blessedearth.org and join our community of Good Stewards. Explore the website to find additional ideas for saving water and becoming a better steward of God's creation.

3. We will send encouragements to you, and help you stay on track. We're all in this together, so share your journey. Let us know what was easy, and what was difficult; inspire others with your story!

Today, Lord, help me to:

(pick at least two of the following goals, or come up with your own actions)

- Turn off the faucet while shaving and brushing teeth.
- Cut shower time by at least three minutes.
- Only run the dishwasher and clothes washer when full.
- Memorize at least one Scripture about water (see "Digging Deeper" at the end of this chapter).
- Pray for the millions of people in the world who live without a reliable source of water.

1. _____

2. _____

This week, Lord help me to:

**(pick at least two of the following goals, or
come up with your own actions)**

- Install low-flow showerheads and sink aerators.
- Fix leaky faucets and toilets.
- Check to see if I have an older toilet that uses three gallons or more per flush; if so, place several liter bottles filled with water in the tank to displace some of the water.
- Use dishwater to water plants.
- Place at least one Scripture about water in a place that I see often (on my bathroom mirror, next to the kitchen faucet, near the dishwasher or clothes washer).

1. _____

2. _____

_____

❝ *What a thing it is to sit absolutely alone, in the forest, at night, cherished by this wonderful, unintelligible, perfectly innocent speech, the most comforting speech in the world, the talk that rain makes by itself all over the ridges, and the talk of the watercourses everywhere in the hollows. Nobody started it; nobody is going to stop it. It will talk as long as it wants, this rain. As long as it talks, I am going to listen.* **❞**

*—Thomas Merton (1915–1968), Raids on the
Unspeakable, Abbey of Gethsemani*

This month, Lord, help me to:

(pick at least two of the following goals, or
come up with your own actions)

- Make time to sit and appreciate water—whether it's the sound of the rain, the expanse of the ocean, or the flow from your faucet. Praise God!
- Store filtered water in the refrigerator, rather than waiting for tap water to run cold or purchasing bottled water.
- When shaving, collect water while waiting for it to run warm, and use the collected water on houseplants.
- Wear pants and suits several times before washing.
- Purchase a front-load washing machine.
- Compost instead of using the garbage disposal.
- Think before I buy anything, and buy used when possible. Most items use huge quantities of water in the manufacturing process.
- Find out about organizations (such as Charity Water) that help people in poor countries who don't have access to clean water and pray about how I can help.

1. _____

2. _____

_____

❝ *We are deeply worried to see that entire peoples, millions of human beings, have been reduced to destitution and are suffering from hunger and disease because they lack drinking water. In fact, hunger and many diseases are closely linked to drought and water pollution. In places where rain is rare or the sources of water dry up, life becomes more fragile; it fades away to the point of disappearing.* **❞**

—*Pope John Paul II, Speech in Brazil, Lenten Message, 1993*

This year, Lord, help me to:

(pick at least two of the following goals, or come up with your own actions)

- Plant native, drought-resistant plants.
- Water outdoor plants early in the morning or late in the evening to reduce evaporation.
- When I use a hose, put a nozzle on the end so I don't leave water running unnecessarily.
- Check the forecast before I water; don't water if they are calling for rain.
- Naturalize part of my yard, so it doesn't need watering at all.
- Install rain barrels or cisterns to collect water off my roof.
- Use drip irrigation rather than sprinklers to water the garden.
- Use mulch to prevent evaporation in the garden.
- Build up my garden soil with compost and organic matter to hold moisture.
- Plant vegetables close together to provide shade and avoid moisture loss.
- Allow my grass to grow longer. Cutting it short encourages growth, which requires more water.
- When cutting the lawn, leave the clippings on the ground.
- Place an insulated cover over swimming pools when not in use.
- When cleaning outside, use a broom instead of a power washer.

Digging Deeper: *What Scripture Says About Water*

According to the first creation story in Genesis, the earth itself was formed by God out of the waters. "In the beginning when God created the heavens and the earth, the earth was a formless void and darkness covered the face of the deep, while a wind from God swept over the face of the waters." *(Genesis 1:1–2)* God first separates the waters above from the waters below, then creates the earth out of the waters. Once the earth is formed, He places all living things, including humans, on earth—all dependent on water for continued life.

Just as the earth is born out of the waters, so is each individual. Not only do babies develop for nine months in the womb's water, but each of us is called to be reborn as Christians in the living waters. As Jesus said to Nicodemus, "No one can enter the kingdom of God without being born of water and Spirit." *(John 3:5)*

The miracles of creation and life are just two of the many miracles associated with water. The Flood and the subsequent redemption *(Genesis 6–9)*, the preservation of the infant Moses *(Exodus 2)*, the plagues in Egypt *(Exodus 7–10)*, the dividing of the Red Sea *(Exodus 14)*, the water from the rock *(Exodus 17)*, the dividing of the Jordan River *(Joshua 3)*, Elijah and the drought *(1 Kings 17–18)*, the consumption of Elijah's water-drenched altar *(1 Kings 18)*, Jesus turning water into wine *(John 2)*, the great catches of fish *(Luke 5; John 21)*, Jesus walking on water *(Matthew 14)*, and Jesus calming the stormy seas *(Mark 4)* show God using water as evidence of His presence and power.

Scripture repeatedly reminds us to be grateful for the miracle of water in our daily lives. Water is a gift from God: "He does great things and unsearchable, marvelous things without number. He gives rain on the earth and sends waters on the fields." *(Job 5:9–10)*

Many Psalms tell us not to take water for granted, but to cherish it. In Psalm 107, Psalm 65, and Psalm 104, we are reminded that God not only provides water for humans but for all of His creatures: "You make springs gush forth in the valleys; they flow between the hills, giving drink to every wild animal; the wild asses quench their thirst. By the streams the birds of the air have their habitation; they sing among the branches. From your lofty abode you water the mountains; the earth is satisfied with the fruit of your work." *(Psalm 104:10–13)*

Perhaps the greatest reason we should cherish water is that water is a symbol of God. God is the "drink from the river" and the "fountain of life" *(Psalm 36:8–9)*. He is the "living water" that never leaves us thirsty *(John 4:10–14)*. God cleanses us through the waters of baptism: "wash yourselves; make yourselves clean." Indeed, one way we can "cease to do evil, learn to do good; seek justice, rescue the oppressed, defend the orphan" *(Isaiah 1:16–17)* is by becoming better stewards of God's life-giving waters.

Adapted with permission from *The Gospel According to the Earth: Why the Good Book Is a Green Book* by Matthew Sleeth (HarperOne, 2010)

❝ *How great is God—beyond our understanding!...*
He draws up the drops of water, which distill as rain
to the streams; the clouds pour down their moisture
and abundant showers fall on mankind. **❞**

—Job 36:26–28 (NIV)

Session 3 Soil

Session Summary

❝ *I am the vine; you are the branches. If a man remains in me and I in him, he will bear much fruit; apart from me you can do nothing.* **❞**

—*John 15:5 (NIV)*

One of the few parables that Jesus overtly explains is the story of the four soils. As we sow seeds, some fall on the path and are eaten by birds; these are the truths that we hear and the devil takes away. The seeds that fall on the rock are truths that sprout, but wither in hard times because they have no root to sustain them. The seeds that grow up with the thorns are eventually choked out; these represent the cares and the emails and the current events that distract us from God. But the seeds that fall onto good soil yield good fruit in abundance—this is the soil that pleases God.

God wants us to grow in our faith, like trees planted in good soil. Trees are mentioned hundreds of times in the Bible. Wherever there's a tree, a branch, a bush, a vine, or a stick on the page, it's a safe bet that God is at work. At the center of the Garden of Eden are two of the most important trees: the Tree of Life and the Tree of Knowledge. God speaks to Moses through a burning bush. Moses holds up a branch to part the Red Sea. Abraham meets the angels under the oaks of Mamre. Deborah holds court under a palm tree. Nathaniel prays beneath the trees when Jesus calls him to be a disciple.

All of these scriptural references to trees, branches, and vines call us to bear fruit in our lives. Jesus describes the fruit of the Spirit as love, joy, peace, patience, kindness, goodness, faithfulness, gentleness, and self-control. When our actions are filled with the fruit of the Spirit, we are in a right relationship with God, our neighbors, and His creation. Jesus is the vine, and we are the branches. Apart from Him, we cannot become better stewards of creation; but with Him, all things are possible.

Reflections on Soil

In my women's spiritual group, we decided to each write down a question for everyone to answer as a way of getting to know each other better. One member of the group wrote: "Describe a miracle in your life."

What a great invitation! I listened as the young woman seated to my right described her miracle. She had been raised in an affluent community where everyone in her neighborhood had gardens, but no one she knew grew food. Just out of college and equipped with a degree in finance, something (or Someone) led her to purchase a five-inch tomato plant. Moving the plant to her patio, she wondered how that weak little stem could ever support a full-grown tomato. Every day after work, she sat on the patio and stared at the plant. She continued to watch in amazement as the plant grew and developed flowers. Soon, little green balls appeared, grew ever larger, and then slowly blushed crimson.

Watching that tomato plant grow changed her heart. In awe of God's creation and no longer desiring the career she had prepared for in banking, she started learning about a totally different form of currency. In a series of conversations, her pastor discussed ways she could live out her faith not just on Sundays, but in her everyday life. These two revolutionary ideas—that people could work to grow their own food and grow their own faith—merged.

She learned as much as she could about sustainable agriculture, quit her job, and interned with an organic farmer. Over the last five years, she's worked for environmental nonprofits and started community gardens.

God used one tomato plant to change a life—now that's what I call miraculous.

—*Nancy Sleeth*

Adapted with permission from *Go Green, Save Green: A Simple Guide to Saving Time, Money, and God's Green Earth* by Nancy Sleeth (Tyndale, 2009)

Session Notes: Soil

As you watch the third film session on **Soil**, feel free to use the following page to jot down notes, thoughts, and questions.

Hope Begins with a Changed Heart

1 In the opening of the film, Dr. Sleeth states, "When I was in medical school, we were taught to look for patterns. Recognizing patterns in symptoms and diseases helped us be better doctors and heal our patients." What behaviors or trends in our twenty-first century lifestyle are harming the earth?

2 "God has a special relationship with all of creation, but especially with trees." Reflect on one or more events in the Bible that involve trees, branches, or vines (examples: the Tree of Life, the burning bush, the cross). What do they teach us?

❝ *Men will become poor because they will not have a love for trees…. If you don't love trees, you don't love God.* **❞**

—*Nikephoros of Chios (1750–1821)*

3

What do you believe Nikephoros meant when he said that people would become impoverished by their lack of love for trees?

❝ *Even if you are old, you must plant. Just as you found trees planted by others, you must plant them for your children.* **❞**

—*4th century writing*

Planting a tree is an investment in the future; the trees you enjoy today are gifts from prior generations. Describe a tree that has given you joy. Are you planting trees for future generations?

5 ❝ *Jesus is being clear. We're being called to bear fruit ... the fruit of the Spirit.* ❞

—*Dr. Matthew Sleeth*

What does the fruit of the Spirit—qualities such as self-control, love, and kindness—have to do with becoming a better steward of God's creation?

6 ❝ *When I chose to follow Jesus, He made it clear that I needed to make some changes in my life. And if you choose to [become a follower of Jesus], you've got to make changes, too.* ❞

—*Dr. Matthew Sleeth*

What changes in your life have you made since becoming a follower of Jesus?

❝ *The seriousness of ecological degradation lays bare the depth of man's moral crisis.... Simplicity, moderation and discipline, as well as the spirit of sacrifice, must become a part of everyday life.* **❞**

—**Pope John Paul II (1920–2005), Peace with God, Peace with Creation**

7

One leader warned Dr. Sleeth that he should never mention the word "sacrifice" when speaking about caring for creation. Sacrifice, however, is the cornerstone of our faith. How can sacrifice become a key component of solving some of our environmental problems?

❝ *People will often ask, 'What was the hardest thing to give up?' They expect me to say 'my car' or 'my house' or 'my paycheck.' But, for me, it was my social status.* **❞**

—**Dr. Matthew Sleeth**

8

If you simplified your life, what would be the hardest thing for you to give up?

9 **❝** *The most beautiful part was that one by one, my wife and my children all became followers of Christ. We were on the same page, serving the same God with the same priorities. We found that the fewer possessions we owned, the less things owned us.* **❞**

—*Dr. Matthew Sleeth*

How are "things" keeping you from a Christ-focused life?

The average school-aged child spends six hours and twenty minutes in front of a screen each day, but less than half an hour a week in unstructured play outdoors. What effect do you believe this is having on the next generation?

10

ʟʟ *Reading about nature is fine, but if a person walks in the woods and listens carefully, he can learn more than what is in books, for they speak with the voice of God.* **ʟʟ**

—*George Washington Carver (early 1860s–1943)*

11

Recall a time when you found peace or solace by being in nature. Describe it. How can being alone in nature bring us closer to God?

A Changed Heart = A Changed Life

I didn't always love gardening. I grew up in the suburbs and, every spring, my dad had a load of steaming mulch dumped in our driveway. It was the children's job to shovel the mulch into the wheelbarrow and spread it evenly around the trees and bushes. When we finally scraped up the last shovelful, our yard looked beautiful … but gardening had sunk to the bottom of my list of desired vocations.

By the time I was twelve or thirteen, I'd discovered a way to avoid most outdoor work: my mom would rather weed in the sunshine than be tied to the kitchen, so I traded outside chores for fixing dinner.

I was twenty years old when Matthew and I married—by then I was skillful in the kitchen, but still had no desire to be a gardener. For the first seven years of our marriage, we mostly lived in apartments where gardening was not an option.

My attitude adjustment occurred during Matthew's residency. Our next-door neighbors had been raised in a Mennonite farming community. Thinking it would be fun to grow some of our own food with our young children, we decided to start a garden together.

The house where we lived already had a small garden plot adjacent to the garage. I planted easy-to-grow carrots, tomatoes, radishes, and peas— not enough to feed a family, but the look on our son Clark's face when he pulled up his first carrot was payment enough for my effort. Later we added corn and squash in my neighbor's plot. Growing food fit my frugal nature, and it got me out of the house. I was hooked.

After Matthew finished his residency, we moved to northern New England. Although the growing season there is short, people plant magnificent perennial gardens. Thanks to neighbors who offered to give me divisions from their plants, I was able to plant a spring-to-fall succession of blooms. Next to my vegetable garden, I planted blueberry bushes and a small orchard.

The biggest shift in my gardening practices, however, came when we built our house in New Hampshire.

There are 30 million acres of "mowable" lawns in the U.S., and 66 million U.S. households own at *least* one lawnmower. Altogether, U.S. lawnmowers use 580 million gallons of gasoline each year.

So, instead of planting grass, I sowed two thirds of an acre with wild-flower seed. The field thrived and attracted wildlife—birds, deer, wild turkeys ... and tourists. Strangers stopped to ask if they could photograph and paint the field. Neighbors were invited to pick bouquets. Churches used our wildflowers for special occasions.

Homeowners spend a total of $29 billion annually on professional lawn care.

Two friends helped us construct raised beds for my vegetable garden. The vegetable garden was so successful the first summer that we decided to double it in size the next, and double it again the next. By the third year, we were growing enough potatoes, carrots, onions, and tomatoes to last year-round. Clark and Emma often weeded with me in the early morning. Matthew used our pressure cooker to can our bounty. It was a family enterprise.

When we moved to Kentucky, one of my first priorities was preparing a small organic garden on the south side of our house. We've used the garden for teaching college students basic gardening skills, from preparing the earth all the way to harvest. Yet sometimes I still feel very much like an amateur gardener, with so much yet to learn.

Matthew's family grew and raised the majority of their food for economic reasons, so for a long while, gardening brought back not-so-fond memories for him of picking potato bugs off plants. But recently, Matthew has joined me in the garden. Come evening, when we work in comfortable silence among the rows, it feels like Paradise restored: just as God intended, husband and wife together, tending and caring for the Lord's earthly garden.

—Nancy Sleeth

Adapted with permission from *Go Green, Save Green: A Simple Guide to Saving Time, Money, and God's Green Earth* (Tyndale, 2009)

Good Steward Action Plan: Soil

Instructions

1. Pick two or more new actions from the suggested lists to commit to today, this week, this month, and this year—or come up with your own way to care for the earth.
2. Go to blessedearth.org and join our community of Good Stewards. Explore the website to find additional ideas for becoming a better steward of God's creation.
3. We will send you encouragement throughout the year and help you stay on track with your goals. We're all in this together, so share your journey. Let us know what was easy, and what was difficult; inspire others with your story!

Today, Lord, help me to:

(pick at least two of the following goals, or come up with your own actions)

- Spend at least five minutes seeing only what God has created. If necessary, I will close off my field of vision to a six-inch patch of nature, and meditate on His goodness. "Be still, and know that I am God."
- Research organizations (Floresta, Restoring Eden Project, Heifer Project) that plant trees in developing countries and ask God how I can help.
- Find out about local parks and outdoor activities that my family might enjoy.
- Check the weather forecast and schedule a good night for viewing stars.
- Take a walk outdoors.

1. _____

2. _____

This week, Lord help me to:

(pick at least two of the following goals, or
come up with your own actions)

- Purchase local, organic food.
- Hang a bird feeder in a tree near my window.
- Do something out of the ordinary outdoors, such as get up early
  to take a sunrise walk, feed the ducks in my local park, practice
  skipping stones across a stream, or spread a blanket on the ground at
  night and look up at the stars.
- Bring a bag when I go for a walk and pick up any trash I see.
- Look into faith-based environmental organizations—such as
  Blessed Earth, A Rocha, and the Evangelical Environmental
  Network—and pray about how I can get involved.

1. _____

2. _____

_____

ᴮᴮ *One guy knocked on our door and asked if he could
pick some flowers from our wildflower meadow because
he'd forgotten to get his wife an anniversary gift. We've
had two guys paint pictures of our yard, and several
others have photographed it. I get to bring bouquets to
people all summer long, and the retired teacher next door
regularly picks flowers for church dinners. I'm pretty sure
that man who forgot his anniversary would have gotten
a frown instead of kiss if we'd had a normal lawn.* **ᴮᴮ**

—**Emma Sleeth, daughter of Matthew and Nancy**

Adapted with permission from *It's Easy Being Green: One Student's Guide to Serving God and
Saving the Planet* (Zondervan/Youth Specialties, 2008)

This month, Lord, help me to:

(pick at least two of the following goals, or come up with your own actions)

- Support local farms and CSAs (community supported agriculture).
- Take plants into work and school. They'll freshen the air while bringing joy to others.
- Educate myself on ways to protect God's creation:
  - Conserve open space (www.nature.org)
  - Support natural habitats (www.worldwildlife.org)
  - Save national parks (www.parktrust.org)
- Engage in an activity outside that I enjoyed as a child—swinging on a swing set, rolling down a hill, playing catch, climbing a tree, horseback riding.
- Go on a picnic.
- Plan a camping trip or overnight visit to a park.

1. _____

2. _____

This year, Lord, help me to:

(pick at least two of the following goals, or come up with your own actions)

- Plant shade trees and fruit-bearing bushes and trees in my yard or neighborhood.
- Start a vegetable garden.
- Mow the grass with a push mower or solar mower.
- Rake leaves instead of collecting them with a blower or mower.
- Start a compost pile.
- Mow the lawn lower and less frequently.
- Reduce the size of the yard—let the backyard go natural.
- Plant wildflowers or native plants.
- Can, freeze, or dry in-season fruits and vegetables.
- Avoid the use of chemicals and pesticides in the yard.
- Organize a church or community garden, and donate produce.
- Celebrate Arbor Day.
- Protect community green spaces and parks.

1. _____

2. _____

_____

❝ *I pray that you're rooted in good soil and that you bear good fruit. I pray that you'll become a giant tree that offers shade and life to everyone around you. I pray that you'd come to love trees just as God loves trees. One day in heaven, we'll sit in the shade of a tree at the foot of God's throne and it will be good.* **❞**

—*Dr. Matthew Sleeth*

Digging Deeper: *What Scripture Says About Soil*

God is pleased by those who care for the soil. Uzziah, a king of Judah who ruled for fifty-two years and was "pleasing in the Lord's sight," was "a man who loved the soil. He had many workers who cared for his farms and vineyards, both on the hillsides and in the fertile valleys." *(2 Chronicles 26:10, NLT)*

Throughout Scripture, good soil is used as an analogy for righteous living. "For as the soil makes the sprout come up and a garden causes seeds to grow, so the Sovereign Lord will make righteousness and praise spring up before all nations." *(Isaiah 61:11, NIV)*

Jesus' parable of the four soils is perhaps the most well-known description of how faith can flourish in good soil, but wither in bad soil. "Listen! A farmer went out to plant some seeds. As he scattered them across his field, some seeds fell on a footpath, and the birds came and ate them. Other seeds fell on shallow soil with underlying rock. The seeds sprouted quickly because the soil was shallow. But the plants soon wilted under the hot sun, and since they didn't have deep roots, they died. Other seeds fell among thorns that grew up and choked out the tender plants. Still other seeds fell on fertile soil, and they produced a crop that was thirty, sixty, and even a hundred times as much as had been planted!" *(Matthew 13:3–8)*

Where there is good soil, the seeds of faith grow. "[Jesus] told them another parable: 'The kingdom of heaven is like a mustard seed, which a man took and planted in his field. Though it is the smallest of all your seeds, yet when it grows, it is the largest of garden plants and becomes a tree, so that the birds of the air come and perch in its branches.'" *(Matthew 13:31–32, NIV)*

Using soil and faith, Jesus heals. "Then he spit on the ground, made mud with the saliva, and spread the mud over the blind man's eyes. He told him, 'Go wash yourself in the pool of Siloam.' So the man went and washed and came back seeing!" *(John 9:6–7)*

Indeed, Jesus is the vine that nourishes the branches that they might bear fruit. "I am the true vine, and my Father is the gardener. He cuts off every branch in me that bears no fruit, while every branch that does bear fruit he prunes so that it will be even more fruitful." *(John 15:1–2, NIV)*

Mary was *not* mistaken at the empty tomb. Jesus is the Gardener.
"'Woman,' he said, 'why are you crying? Who is it you are looking for?' Thinking he was the gardener, she said, 'Sir, if you have carried him away, tell me where you have put him, and I will get him.' Jesus said to her, 'Mary.' She turned toward him and cried out in Aramaic, 'Rabboni!'" *(John 20:15–16, NIV)*

Adapted with permission from *The Gospel According to the Earth: Why the Good Book Is a Green Book* by Matthew Sleeth (HarperOne, 2010)

❝ *When my dad talks to groups about the need to care for creation, he's often asked, 'Isn't this environment thing kind of low on the list of Christian priorities? What if Jesus comes back today?' Dad usually answers by telling a story about the reformer Martin Luther. Apparently, Luther once gave a Sunday morning sermon about the second coming of Christ. He was such a powerful preacher that when his parishioners went home, they all started acting as if Jesus were going to return that afternoon. One man from the church happened to walk by Luther's house and saw him planting a tree. The parishioner was puzzled and asked him if he really believed his own sermon, shouldn't he be doing what he'd want to be doing when Jesus returns? Luther answered that planting a tree was exactly what he wanted to be caught doing when the Lord came back. I'd have to say 'Amen.' If Jesus came back this afternoon, I'd rather be tending to God's beautiful creation than doing just about anything else.* ❞

—*Emma Sleeth*

Adapted with permission from *It's Easy Being Green: One Student's Guide to Serving God and Saving the Planet* by Emma Sleeth (Zondervan/Youth Specialties, 2008)

Session 4
Heavens

Session Summary

❝ *He counts the stars and calls them all by name.
How great is our Lord! His power is absolute! His
understanding is beyond comprehension!* **❞**

—*Psalm 147:4–5 (NLT)*

God created a universe of wonder for us to enjoy. He gave us the sun and
the moon for warmth and light and stars to help us find our way. On the
one hand, these heavenly bodies are reassuring, giving order to our days,
our seasons, and our yearly calendar. On the other hand, they are full of
mystery beyond our comprehension.

Both of these aspects of the night sky teach us about the face of God.
The heavens show us that God cares about every detail of our lives; God
knows the name of every star, just as He knows every hair on our head. At
the same time, the vastness of the heavens reminds us just how small we
are, keeping us humble before our Creator. The universe is filled not only
by stars and solar systems, but by untold billions of galaxies.

When we look up at the night sky, we get a glimpse of just how big God is.
He's a God who can speak galaxies into existence; He can create extravagant, over-the-top beauty in the farthest reaches of space … and provide
the moon to help us find our way home on a dark night. He's with us when
we feel lost and small and scared and alone.

It's not by accident that a star announces the birth of the infant Christ.
And on the last page of the Bible, Christ describes Himself as the "bright
morning star." If you ever begin to think that maybe God's love isn't quite
big enough to save a people or a planet as messed up as we are, stare into
the night sky and—just like Abraham—try to count the stars.

God calls us to trust that He is present in all the mysteries of life. When
we embrace the mystery of the heavens, we begin to understand a little bit
more about the nature of God.

Reflections on Heavens

It's my parents' fault that Matthew and I moved to New England.

For two weeks every August, my family went camping. One summer when I was about eleven or twelve, we camped at Sebago Lake in Maine. What I remember most from that trip were the shooting stars. Every night, we went down to the docks and stared up at the heavens. No Hollywood movie or concert could compete with the free show we watched on those cool, starry nights.

When Matthew and I were first married, I took him to New England to see "real stars." We stayed at a lakeside cottage that belonged to friends of my parents. The stars were even better than I remembered. Matthew was hooked.

After Matthew's residency, we spent a dozen years living in Maine. Many summer nights, we brought blankets out onto the back deck and watched the comets streak across the sky. Often the kids fell asleep there, tucked into sleeping bags. What could be more pleasant and secure than Daddy carrying you in his arms up to bed, all the while dreaming of God's diamonds in the sky?

—*Nancy Sleeth*

Adapted with permission from *Go Green, Save Green: A Simple Guide to Saving Time, Money, and God's Green Earth* (Tyndale, 2009)

Session Notes: Heavens

As you watch the fourth film session on the **Heavens**, feel free to use the following page to jot down notes, thoughts, and questions.

Hope Begins with a Changed Heart

 Dr. Sleeth describes some of his favorite memories looking up at the night sky—as a child, husband, and parent. What memories do you associate with the night sky?

 The heavens also give order to our lives. Describe some of ways that the heavens provide a rhythm to the days, seasons, and yearly calendar of your life.

❝ *When I consider your heavens, the work of your fingers, the moon and the stars, which you have set in place, what is man that you are mindful of him, the son of man that you care for him?* **❞**

—*Psalm 8:3–4 (NIV)*

Can you recall a time when you were awed by the vastness of the night sky? Explain.

4 **❝** *The heavens declare the glory of God; the skies proclaim the work of his hands.* **❞**

—*Psalm 19:1 (NIV)*

What do the heavens teach you about the face of God?

The book of Job contains the longest soliloquy by God in the Bible. God asks Job, "Can you direct the movement of the stars—binding the cluster of the Pleiades or loosening the cords of Orion? Can you direct the sequence of the seasons or guide the Bear with her cubs across the heavens? Do you know the laws of the universe? Can you use them to regulate the earth?" What does this passage teach us about humility?

5

6 **❝** *As the heavens are higher than the earth,*
so are my ways higher than your ways and
my thoughts than your thoughts. **❞**

—*Isaiah 55:9 (NIV)*

What is the prophet Isaiah trying to teach us about our relationship to God and his creation?

---

7 **❝** *Nothing in creation has erred from the path of God's*
purpose for it, save only man. Sun, moon, stars, water,
air, none of these has swerved from their order, but,
knowing the Word as their Maker and their King, remained
as they were made. Men alone, having rejected what is
good, have invented nothings instead of the truth. **❞**

—*Athanasius (297–373), On the Incarnation of the Word of God*

In relation to our current stewardship of God's creation, in what ways have we "swerved" and "rejected what is good"?

8

❝ *So that you may become blameless and pure, children of God without fault in a crooked and depraved generation, in which you shine like stars in the universe as you hold out the word of life ...* **❞**

—Philippians 2:15–16 (NIV)

In addition to inspiring awe, the heavens can offer hope. In context of creation care, how can we "shine like stars in the universe" amidst "a crooked and depraved generation"?

A Changed Heart = A Changed Life

A friend of Emma's recently told me that he rarely looks to see if the stars are visible at night. "I just don't think about it," he said. "My dad said he and his friends could find all the constellations and would play late into the night under the stars, but I didn't grow up that way."

This young man is not alone. When I spoke at a college in Texas, I asked how many of the students in the audience had seen the Milky Way. Only a few hands went up. I have found this to be true in colleges all over the country:

Three fourths of Americans grow up never having seen the Milky Way.

In the last two centuries, we've obscured the Milky Way that Abraham, Isaac, Jacob, Jesus, and Paul all knew so well by filling the night sky with manmade light.

While artificial light certainly has benefits, it also has consequences—something called light pollution. Light pollution is caused in large part by poor lighting design—artificial light shining upward and outward toward the sky rather than focusing downward, where it is needed.

From space, all of Europe and Japan and most of America can be seen as a glowing dome of light.

In satellite photos taken at night, we can see that at least two thirds of humanity lives under light-polluted skies.

Here on earth, even on the clearest nights, most city residents can no longer view the stars. Instead, they have grown accustomed to a ubiquitous orange haze, while the glorious heavens created by God continue to shine, undisturbed and unheeded.

When we disrupt God's natural rhythm of light and dark, the migration, reproduction, and feeding of life on earth is affected. Along the coasts, sea turtles have a harder time finding darkened beaches for nesting. Frogs and toads living near highways artificially made as much as a million times brighter than normal have their nighttime breeding songs thrown out of kilter. Whole flocks of winged creatures exhaust themselves trying to escape the maze of city lights.

Artificial light also harms humans. Our regular pattern of waking and sleeping—called circadian rhythms—are fundamental to mental and physical well-being. As an emergency room physician, I often worked twenty-four-hour shifts. ER docs are not alone—today nearly one fifth of the world population works in shifts. The resulting lack of regular sleep and rest is not conducive to a healthy home life, or a healthy body. Hypertension, peptic ulcer disease, cardiovascular mortality, higher incidences of work-related accidents and car accidents, depression, drug and alcohol abuse, and higher divorce rates are more common in shift workers. Life expectancy for shift workers is reduced by as much as four years. Is our twenty-four-hour productivity quota really worth the toll?

By short-circuiting our sensitivity to God's patterns of light and dark, we are blindly experimenting with human health as well as the health of every living creature on earth. But here's the good news:

Of all the forms of pollution facing the world today, light pollution is probably the most easily fixed.

Simple changes in lighting design and installation translates to immediate reductions in the amount of light we pour out into the atmosphere. As a bonus, these changes also save us energy. Hundreds of communities throughout the U.S. now use covered street fixtures that light only the ground below rather than wastefully shining it in all directions. At home, porch lights that are tucked into ceilings and outdoor motion detectors can ensure safety while reducing waste.

Light pollution (and air pollution in general) interferes with stargazing. But something else often gets in the way: we are often so worn out from our busy schedules that we don't take time to connect with the natural world. Slow down. Shut off the TV, close the laptop, and linger outdoors in the evenings for a change. Switch off the porch lights, spread a blanket on the lawn, and try to count the stars, just as Abraham did. As you gaze upward, you cannot help but be filled with humility and the wonder of God's creation.

—*Dr. Matthew Sleeth*

Good Steward Action Plan: Heavens

Instructions

1. Pick two or more new actions from the suggested lists to commit to today, this week, this month, and this year—or come up with your own ways to curb light pollution and conserve electricity.
2. Go to blessedearth.org and join our community of Good Stewards. Explore the website to find additional ideas for becoming a better steward of God's creation.
3. We will send you encouragement throughout the year and help you stay on track with your goals. We're all in this together, so share your journey. Let us know what was easy, and what was difficult; inspire others with your story!

Today, Lord, help me to:

(pick at least two of the following goals, or come up with your own actions)

- Turns lights off in rooms that are not in use.
- Direct light to where it is needed instead of flooding general areas; use a lamp instead of an overhead light for reading or enjoying a meal; use less light wherever possible.
- Turn off all lights before going to bed.
- Spend a few minutes outside tonight, looking at the stars; ask God to reveal how I can become a better steward of His creation.

1. _____

2. _____

This week, Lord help me to:

(pick at least two of the following goals, or come up with your own actions)

- Reserve activities that require a lot of lighting, such as painting walls, artwork, sewing, and cleaning to the daytime hours when the sun provides a light source instead of trying to do work under intense lights at night.
- Install motion detectors for outdoor lighting.
- Consider installing motion detector lights inside, especially in rooms where the lights are left on often.
- Use dimmer LED nightlights instead of regular incandescent bulbs.
- At night, keep the light inside and don't let the glow out; shut the blinds, draw the drapes, and dim the switches when possible.

1. _____

2. _____

_____

❝ *Last summer, our daughter Emma pretty much became obsessed by the stars and decided to pitch a tent in the backyard. Her small, one-person tent has a window in the top for viewing the night sky. She made the tent cozy with a mat, sleeping bag, a few books, and a flashlight—and ended up sleeping outside the whole summer. Falling asleep week after week under the open sky and waking up with the sun shining on her face gave Emma a new appreciation for God's rhythms.* **❞**

—*Nancy Sleeth*

This month, Lord, help me to:

(pick at least two of the following goals, or come up with your own actions)

- Look for lighting that directs light down where you need it rather than in all directions.
- Carpool, use public transportation, and combine trips to reduce smog.
- Install energy-efficient bulbs, dry clothes on the line, and adjust the thermostat by at least three degrees to cut back on electricity usage.
- Install thick, tight blinds on the windows to both save energy and prevent the light from being seen from the outside of the house.
- Look at the stars through a telescope.

Examples of Some Common Lighting Fixtures

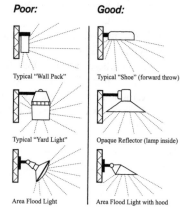

Poor: *Good:*

Typical "Wall Pack"   Typical "Shoe" (forward throw)

Typical "Yard Light"   Opaque Reflector (lamp inside)

Area Flood Light   Area Flood Light with hood

1. _____

2. _____

This year, Lord, help me to:

(pick at least two of the following goals, or come up with your own actions)

- Consider turning my porch lights off altogether, or replacing them with LED units.
- Spread the word about light pollution to my family and friends, and recruit others to protect the night sky.
- Write a letter to my city council suggesting that they change their streetlights so that all the floodlights point down.
- Sleep under the stars, like our ancestors did. Make it a romantic evening, or plan a fun family outing. (Camping out in the backyard is easy and a great way to admire the stars.)

1. _____

2. _____

_____

❝ *Dear heavenly Father, please help me become a better steward of Your creation, on earth as it is in heaven. As I stare in awe at the night sky, fill my heart with humility and wonder. I praise You for the daily miracle of light and darkness, work and rest. Thank You most of all for the gift of Your Son, the Bright Morning Star, in whose name I pray.* **❞**

—*Nancy Sleeth*

Digging Deeper: *What Scripture Says About the Heavens*

God created the heavens. God made two great lights—the greater light to govern the day and the lesser light to govern the night. He also made the stars. *(Genesis 1:16)*

In His covenant, God promises Abraham that his descendants will be as numerous as the stars. "He took him outside and said, 'Look up at the heavens and count the stars—if indeed you can count them.' Then he said to him, 'So shall your offspring be.'" *(Genesis 15:5)*

Unlike other surrounding cultures, the Israelites did not worship the sun, moon, and stars; rather, they understood them to be gifts from the Creator and eternal reminders of His glory. "And when you look up to the sky and see the sun, the moon and the stars—all the heavenly array—do not be enticed into bowing down to them and worshiping things the LORD your God has apportioned to all the nations under heaven." *(Deuteronomy 4:19)*

The heavens keep our all-too-human pride in check. "On what were its footings set, or who laid its cornerstone—while the morning stars sang together and all the angels shouted for joy?" *(Job 38:6–7)* "Can you bind the beautiful Pleiades? Can you loose the cords of Orion? Can you bring forth the constellations in their seasons or lead out the Bear with its cubs?" *(Job 38:31–32)*

They remind us of our place in the universe. "When I consider your heavens, the work of your fingers, the moon and the stars, which you have set in place, what is man that you are mindful of him, the son of man that you care for him?" *(Psalm 8:3–4)*

They literally and spiritually keep us on track. "The moon marks off the seasons, and the sun knows when to go down." *(Psalm 104:19)*

God knows all of the stars by name, just as He knows and loves each of us. "He determines the number of the stars and calls them each by name." *(Psalm 147:4)*

When we are in God's will, we shine as brightly as the heavens. "Those who are wise will shine like the brightness of the heavens, and those who lead many to righteousness, like the stars for ever and ever." *(Daniel 12:23)*

Jesus shines brightest of all, a light for all humankind. "There he was transfigured before them. His face shone like the sun, and his clothes became as white as the light." *(Matthew 17:2)*

Like Jesus, we are to share God's light throughout the world. "[S]hine like stars in the universe as you hold out the word of life—in order that I may boast on the day of Christ that I did not run or labor for nothing." *(Philippians 2:14–16)*

God is the eternal light and Jesus is the lamp of truth and salvation. "[T]he glory of God gives it light, and the Lamb is its lamp." *(Revelation 21:23)*

Adapted with permission from *The Gospel According to the Earth: Why the Good Book Is a Green Book*, by Dr. Matthew Sleeth (HarperOne, 2010)

Session 5
Animals

Session Summary

❝ But ask the animals, and they will teach you, or the birds of the air, and they will tell you; or speak to the earth, and it will teach you, or let the fish of the sea inform you. Which of all these does not know that the hand of the LORD has done this? In his hand is the life of every creature and the breath of all mankind. ❞

—*Job 12:7–10 (NIV)*

God is in the life business. It's his desire that the sky and the air teem with creatures. He allowed Adam the privilege and responsibility of naming each creature, and He entrusts us with their stewardship. We are charged with caring for and protecting the habitats they depend upon for survival.

Even though God has entrusted us with stewardship of animals, the reality is that He still holds the deed to the planet. It's therefore not surprising that compassion for animals is associated with godly people, such as Noah, Moses, Rebekah, and Laban. In contrast, people such as Levi and Simeon are cursed not only because they are cruel to humans, but because they are cruel to animals.

Jesus, our model for compassion, is called the Good Shepherd and "the firstborn of all creatures." He's born in a manger surrounded by animals, and His first visitors are shepherds who have come to see the Lamb of the World. After Jesus is baptized, the Holy Spirit descends upon Him like a dove. Christ gets His taxes out of the mouth of a fish and He rides into Jerusalem on the back of a colt. There's an intimate connection between Jesus and God's creatures.

As followers of Christ, we should love what God loves. When we care about every bird in the sky as deeply as our Father, He is pleased.

Reflections on Animals

It's been a dreadfully hot summer, so I haven't gone on my favorite hike down to the river very often in the last couple of months. But today, the temperature (if not the humidity) dropped a bit, so I decided to make the journey. My glasses fogged up repeatedly, and some much-needed rain dampened my body and clothes, but my soul, as always, was lifted by this time in God's creation.

On this hike the easy part comes first; I hike down for the view. The view is not some grand vista—just a gently moving river. Always—always!—I find the river to be quietly comforting.

Deep in prayer today, I was startled on my way back up the hill, not by the flock of birds or silent deer that I sometimes disturb, but by the buzz of a bumblebee darting around my head. In between my footsteps, muffled by leafy carpets, I heard the starlings singing. They seemed to be saying, "This is God's woods; not yours, not mine."

I have read arguments by some academicians that animals know, but man knows that he knows. In other words, it's our ability to reflect on what we know that makes us more intellectually sophisticated than the squirrels I heard chattering above me in the woods.

And yet, though we are "smarter," animals have much to teach us. Watching those squirrels jump from branch to branch reminds me that every step I take is no less a leap of faith. The squirrels' seemingly impossible acrobatics are only made possible by the very same hand that holds me up every moment of every day. We, like these forest creatures, must place our ultimate trust in God, just as our offspring trust in us.

The walk in the woods teaches me what animals—and children—instinctively know: that God is fully present all around us, if only we pause long enough to see.

—Nancy Sleeth

Adapted with permission from *Go Green, Save Green: A Simple Guide to Saving Time, Money, and God's Green Earth* (Tyndale, 2009)

Session Notes: Animals

As you watch the fifth film session on **Animals**, feel free to use the following page to jot down notes, thoughts, and questions.

Hope Begins with a Changed Heart

 ❝ *Nothing is without order and purpose in the animal kingdom; each animal bears the wisdom of the Creator and testifies of Him.* **❞**

—*John Climacus (509–603)*

What does the animal kingdom teach us about the Creator?

 Dr. Sleeth says that we are "given dominion of animals, which implies a tremendous amount of responsibility." Have you ever been given dominion over an animal, such as a pet? What did you learn from that the responsibility?

> **" A righteous man cares for the needs of his animal,
> but the kindest acts of the wicked are cruel. "**
>
> —*Proverbs 12:10 (NIV)*

Throughout Scripture, God expresses His desire for us to care for animals. On the Sabbath day, God commanded the Israelites to give their animals rest (Exodus 2:10). In the year of rest for the land, they were to allow livestock and wild animals to eat from their fallow fields (Exodus 23:11; Leviticus 25:7). How do our actions harm the habitats that animals need in order to survive?

4 God commanded the Israelites to help when a ox or donkey had fallen over, or was carrying a burden too heavy for it to bear (Exodus 23:5; Deuteronomy 22:4). In addition, livestock were also allowed to eat as they worked (Deuteronomy 25:4). Finally, God says to us in Proverbs 27:23: "Be sure you know the condition of your flocks, give careful attention to your herds." Most of us are not shepherds or farmers today, but we can still show respect for animals. How can our purchasing power help animals be treated fairly?

God promises a long life to those who will watch over wild birds (Deuteronomy 22:6–7). In Job 38:41, God says that He hears the newborn ravens crying to Him for food. Jesus explains that God supplies food for the wild birds and that not one sparrow falls to the ground without Him noticing (Matthew 6:26; 10:29). What can these scriptural references to birds teach us?

6 John Stott says that we can learn much about God by placing a bird feeder in our yard. What can we learn from observing birds?

❝ *Compassion, in which all ethics must take root, can only attain its full breadth and depth if it embraces all living creatures and does not limit itself to humankind.* **❞**

—*Albert Schweitzer (1875–1965)*

Have you ever seen someone being cruel to an animal? As stewards of creation, why does this upset us?

A Changed Heart = A Changed Life

Open spaces are important for the survival of all of God's creatures. As stewards of God's creation, it is important for us to preserve the habitats that animals need to survive.

We live in an interrelated, interconnected world. To get our 99-cent burgers at the fast-food drive-through, for example, we cut down South American rainforests so our cattle can graze. As a consequence, with no tree roots to hold down the topsoil, the land becomes barren in just a few years and poverty increases. The air grows more polluted because there are no trees to cleanse the air. Without clouds forming over South America or rain falling on Africa, droughts worsen, leading to widespread hunger and starvation. These unintended consequences hurt poor people first and hardest; in addition, they devastate indigenous animal populations.

Underlying these problems is the belief that undeveloped land is of little value. As followers of Christ, all of creation has value. Moreover, Christians are instructed to love what God loves. God loves every sparrow and every lamb. If we value what God values, then we will learn to care for and preserve all of His creation.

No matter where you live, you can help create a nature preserve. Whether you are the steward of a 100-acre farm, a suburban backyard, a townhouse sliver of garden, or a high-rise balcony, animals need food, water, and shelter to thrive. Here are some ways you can help:

Food—Everyone needs to eat, even animals. One of the best investments we ever made is the two bird feeders we hung near our front window. The birds that visit have given us countless hours of enjoyment. You can also feed wildlife by including seeds from a plant, berries, nectar, foliage and twigs, nuts, fruits, sap, pollen, and suet in your garden plans.

Water—Wildlife need sources of clean water for many purposes, including drinking, bathing, and reproduction. Water sources include birdbaths, puddling areas for butterflies, and ponds or rain gardens. If you set up a birdbath, be sure to change the water two to three times per week during warm weather when mosquitoes are breeding, so that any eggs laid in the water don't have time to hatch.

Shelter—Wildlife needs places to hide from people, predators, and inclement weather. Shrubs, thickets, and brush piles provide great hiding places within their bushy leaves and thorns—and a safe place for wildlife to raise their young. Consider making a birdhouse for the types of birds you would like to attract to your habitat. Attracting pollinators, such as bats and bees, can also be beneficial to your garden.

Pesticides and Fertilizers—When we use chemicals on our lawns and gardens, we harm wildlife. If it's harmful to cats and dogs and wildlife, it can't be great for humans either. Many of the chemicals that we use on the lawn and garden end up being ingested by animals, and ultimately enter our food chain.

William McDonough, the dean of green architecture, measures the success of any project by the number of songbirds that remain when he is done. As followers of Christ, perhaps it's time for us to measure the beauty of our lawns and gardens by the birds and other wildlife they shelter, just as God shelters us.

—*Nancy Sleeth*

Good Steward Action Plan: Animals

Instructions

1. Pick two or more new actions from the suggested lists to commit to today, this week, this month, and this year—or come up with your own way to care for animals.
2. Go to blessedearth.org and join our community of Good Stewards. Explore the website to find additional ideas for becoming a better steward of God's creation.
3. We will send encouragements to you, and help you stay on track. We're all in this together, so share your journey. Let us know what was easy, and what was difficult; inspire others with your story!

Today, Lord, help me to:

(pick at least two of the following goals, or come up with your own actions)

- Pray for the well-being of all of God's creatures, and for clarity about how I can live in harmony with them.
- Go for a walk in a park or nature preserve.
- Spend time quietly in nature observing animals.
- Meditate on Mark 16:15: "He said to them, 'Go in to the whole world and proclaim the gospel to every creature.'"
- Memorize a Scripture, such as Psalm 145:9, "The LORD is good to all, compassionate to every creature."

1. _____

2. _____

This week, Lord help me to:

(pick at least two of the following goals, or come up with your own actions)

- Eat at least one more meatless meal than usual.
- Avoid meat, eggs, and poultry raised by factory farms. Instead, seek out local, small farmers who raise animals compassionately.
- Learn about an endangered species and do something to help.
- Hang a bird feeder near a window. Black oil sunflower seed is a favorite of many seed-eating species.
- Look at the fertilizers that I normally use on my lawn and investigate if I can use less harmful substitutes.

1. _____

2. _____

ff *Matthew calls our bird feeders the best entertainment that money can buy. I consider them a priceless stress buster. Several times a day I find myself sitting near the bird feeder, pausing to simply watch God's winged creatures. Observing the birds through a thin sheet of windowpane draws me out of my daily concerns and into God's eternal kingdom. How can I question the existence of a benevolent, gracious Creator when a cardinal or black capped chickadee is just inches away?* **"**

—*Nancy Sleeth*

This month, Lord, help me to:

**(pick at least two of the following goals, or
come up with your own actions)**

- Hang a bird feeder near a window. Black oil sunflower seed is a favorite of many seed-eating species.
- Provide a suet feeder for woodpeckers and other insect-eating birds. (You can make your own suet or buy blocks of suet from a wild bird store. Typically suet blocks are placed in a wire cage that hangs on the side of a tree. Do not put suet out in warm weather or it will go rancid.)
- Start a hummingbird feeder. (To make hummingbird food, dissolve one part white sugar in four parts hot water. Boil the water if you plan to store the nectar in the refrigerator. Let the solution cool to room temperature before putting it in your feeder. You can store homemade nectar for up to a week in the refrigerator.)
- Set up a birdbath.
- Hang a bat house.
- Get involved with an organization that preserves animal habitats, such as the Nature Conservancy or World Wildlife Foundation.
- Look for makeup and other personal care products that are labeled "cruelty free."

1. _____

2. _____

This year, Lord, help me to:

(pick at least two of the following goals, or come up with your own actions)

- Go camping, hiking, and canoeing with children so they will appreciate all of God's creation.
- Plant flowers that attract bee populations.
- Avoid using fertilizers and pesticides in my yard.
- In winter, avoid cutting back dead flowers and foliage, which can serve as valuable food for wildlife. Leave dead stalks, leaves, and seedheads standing to feed wildlife and provide cover.
- Give shelter to wildlife by building a brush pile in an out-of-the-way corner of my property, preferably close to food sources and away from buildings. (Start with a layer of larger limbs and stack branches loosely, adding vegetation and leaves on top to create nooks and crannies of various sizes.)

1. _____

2. _____

_____

" *My prayer is that we truly humble ourselves before God and His creation and strive to learn from His kingdom. May we have the wisdom to know the needs of the creatures that God created, and to care for them as God would care for them. May we learn to love them as God loves us.* **"**

—*Dr. Matthew Sleeth*

Digging Deeper: *What Scripture Says About Animals*

Animals are created by God and belong to Him. "And God said, 'Let the waters bring forth abundantly the moving creatures that hath life, and fowl that may fly above the earth in the open firmament of heaven.' And God created great whales, and every living creature that moveth, which the waters brought forth abundantly, after their kind, and every winged fowl after his kind: and God saw that it was good." *(Genesis 1:20–21, KJV)*

The command to each of the animals to be fruitful and multiply comes before the command to humans to be fruitful and multiply. "And God blessed them, saying, Be fruitful and multiply and fill the waters in the seas, and let fowl multiply in the earth." *(Genesis 1:22, KJV)* This commandment presumes that humankind will preserve a suitable habitat for each kind of animal to thrive.

Humans were given a special stewardship role of responsibility for animals. "And God said, 'Let us make man in our image, after our likeness: and let them have dominion over the fish of the sea, and over the fowl of the air.'" *(Genesis 1:26)*

This responsibility allows the use, but not abuse of animals. We are instructed to know them and to name them. "Out of the ground the LORD formed every beast of the field and every fowl of the air; and brought them unto Adam to see what he would call them." *(Genesis 2:19, KJV)*

The life of Jesus is intertwined with the life of God's creatures. Our Savior was born in the home of sheep and oxen. His ministry begins "with the wild beasts." *(Mark 1:13)* He teaches that it is lawful to rescue a fallen animal on the Sabbath *(Matthew 12)* and that "even the sparrows are not forgotten before God." *(Luke 12:27)* He retrieves taxes from a fish, and brings fish to the net. His triumphant entry into Jerusalem is on a humble donkey *(Matthew 21)*.

It is little wonder, then, that the animal kingdom has much to teach humankind. "But ask the animals, and they will teach you; the birds of the air, and they will tell you; ask the plants of the earth, and they will teach you; and the fish of the sea will declare to you. Who among all these does not know that the hand of the LORD has done this? In his hand is the life of every living thing and the breath of every human being." *(Job 12:7–10)*

We can learn much from even the smallest insects and lowest creatures. "There are four things which are little upon the earth, but they are exceedingly wise: The ants are a people not strong, yet they prepare their food in the summer; the rock badgers are a feeble folk, yet they make their homes in the crags; the locusts have no king, yet they all advance in ranks; the spider skillfully grasps with its leg and it is in king's palaces." *(Proverbs 30:24–28, KJV)*

Jesus teaches us to put our trust in the all-powerful and Almighty God, just as the birds do. "Behold the fowls of the air; for they sow not, neither do they reap; yet your Heavenly Father feedeth them." *(Matthew 6:26–27, KJV)*

In the end, Christ will come to redeem not only humankind, but all of creation. "For God so loved the world, that He gave His only begotten Son, that whosoever believeth in Him should not perish, but have everlasting life." *(John 3:16, KJV)*

Adapted with permission from *The Gospel According to the Earth: Why the Good Book Is a Green Book* by Matthew Sleeth (HarperOne, 2010)

*Session 6
Man*

Session Summary

❝ *The LORD God took the man and put him in the Garden of Eden to work it and take care of it.* **❞**

—*Genesis 2:15*

In Genesis 2:15, God gave us our first job assignment: to tend and protect the Garden. One reason God wants us to take care of the planet is because we can't live without it. Our very survival depends upon the health of the planet.

Taking care of the planet is also a form of giving. Jesus said that the most important kind of giving isn't the kind that seeks recognition. It's about helping people who can't thank you. It's about sacrifice. It's about helping people who aren't even born yet. It's about planting seeds for the future.

Some people think we don't need to take care of the earth because it's all going to be destroyed. Why bother? Jesus could come back tomorrow. And they're right; Jesus could come back tomorrow. But if He doesn't come back for 10,000 years, think about how many people would get to hear the good news. Isn't that reason enough to take care of the world? Wasn't that reason enough for our great-great-grandparents to take care of the world? Someday Jesus will return, but until then, we're told to be the hands and feet of God here on earth.

If we believe in an all-powerful God, maybe we should ask ourselves this question: Why were we born here? Why weren't we just born in heaven? God placed us here because He wants us to choose Him. This life, this time, is a gift—it's a love story. God wants us to say, "I do," not, "I have to."

God designed each of us to be part of a vast body that stretches across time and space and culture. It's called the body of Christ—the church. God didn't leave His church, His body of Christ, floating out in the middle of nowhere. He left it on a planet teeming with life and teeming with hope. God's hope for creation rests in us.

Reflections on Man

All of life on earth is precious—a gift from God. With this gift comes responsibility. Like any gift, it is to be cared for and appreciated.

As a physician, my job was to take care of people. In the emergency room, I saw a lot of what could go wrong with the human body.

It was not my job to judge the patient—only to treat the disease. If a finger was dangling off, I sewed it back on. If children came in with croup, I helped them breathe again. If a drunk got in a fight, I repaired the damage.

Diagnosing a problem and fixing it is good work; I found great satisfaction in sending people out of the ER in better shape than when they came in. But in some cases, I couldn't help thinking that it would have been even better if we could have prevented the damage in the first place.

The same is true for the earth. God is in the life-giving business. He has put all of creation in our care. We are to use the gifts He has given us, but never abuse them. We are to be good stewards of our own lives—and of all life on earth.

—Dr. Matthew Sleeth

Session Notes: Man

As you watch the sixth film session on **Man**, feel free to use the following page to jot down notes, thoughts, and questions.

Hope Begins with a Changed Heart

❝ *God wants us to take care of this planet, but I think there's something even more important to God than birds or trees or clean air. What's even more important to God is you and me and our children and our grandchildren and their grandchildren.* **❞**

—*Dr. Matthew Sleeth*

How does taking care of the planet contribute to the health of our grandchildren?

Dr. Sleeth explains that "taking care of the planet is a form of giving." In what sense is this true? Who are we giving to?

3 *If you believe in an all-powerful God—and I do— maybe you should ask yourself this question: Why was I born here? Why wasn't I just born in heaven?*

—*Dr. Matthew Sleeth*

Why were we born on earth rather than in heaven?

4 *Many people think we don't need to take care of the earth because it's all going to be destroyed.*

—*Dr. Matthew Sleeth*

How would you respond to the "why bother" argument?

❝ *The custody of the garden was given to Adam,
to show that we possess the things which God has
committed to our hands, on the condition that, being
content with the frugal and moderate use of them,
we should take care of what shall remain.* **❞**

—*John Calvin (1509–1564), Commentary on Genesis*

Have recent generations been "content with the frugal and moderate use"
of the earth's resources? Give examples.

6 **❝** *It is not right for us to destroy the world God has given us. He has created everything; as the Bible says, 'The God who made the world and everything in it is the Lord of heaven' (Acts 17:24). To drive to extinction something He has created is wrong. He has a purpose for everything.... We Christians have a responsibility to take the lead in caring for the earth.* **❞**

—*Rev. Billy Graham, Detroit Free Press*

How can Christians take a lead role in "caring for the earth"?

❝ *If my people, which are called by my name, shall humble themselves, and pray, and seek my face, and turn from their wicked ways; then will I hear from heaven, and will forgive their sin, and will heal their land.* **❞**

—*2 Chronicles 7:14*

How does repentance, humility, and seeking the face of God offer hope for the planet?

A Changed Heart = A Changed Life

When we moved from New Hampshire to Kentucky, it gave us the opportunity to simplify by giving away a lot of stuff that was still cluttering our lives. Clothes went to The Salvation Army, art supplies to a kindergarten teacher, books to libraries hit by a hurricane, and tools to a church friend starting a second career as a carpenter.

Since moving in, we've made a number of cost-effective, simple changes to our new, old house. The first thing we did was change all the lightbulbs in the house to compact fluorescents. Matthew also put our stereo and our son's computer on a power switch, eliminating the phantom loads.

We needed to purchase a new washing machine and a refrigerator. At the local home center, I picked out a front-load washer. Using the Energy Star comparison tags, I also found a standard refrigerator that uses 445 kWh per year, much more efficient than others in its class. Matthew lowered the energy use of our new refrigerator even more by turning off the automatic icemaker.

We chose not to purchase a clothes dryer. Instead, Matthew restrung an abandoned clothesline in the backyard. Friends helped us dismantle an unsafe, rickety porch on the back of the house, and Matthew and our son, Clark, built a new one using decking made of recycled soda bottles, thus eliminating the need for toxic stains or paints.

I went to www.freecycle.org and found a free composting bin for the backyard, which eliminates the need to power a garbage disposal in the sink and makes an organic soil booster for the garden. I also used Freecycle to give away our moving boxes and some extra building materials. Thanks to Freecycle, someone else used whatever we didn't need—including the former deck stairs and extra lumber from the deck, which prevented scrap from going into the landfill.

Next, Matthew got busy on the glamorous part of conservation, changing a leaky float valve in the toilet and cutting the water used per flush in half by inserting several bricks and a milk jug filled with water into the toilet tanks. He also changed the showerhead to a low-flow model (purchased at the hardware store for about $5), turned the water heater to its lowest setting, and then put insulation on the accessible basement piping. The insulation looks like black foam tubing and slips around the pipes quite easily. These toilet and shower projects only took a couple of hours and will save both energy and water for years to come.

The old single-pane aluminum windows in the house were a huge area of thermal gain and loss. We could not afford to replace them right away, but I greatly improved their efficiency by making heavy, lined drapes for all the windows. The attic only had three inches of insulation, so we increased it to R–60. (The higher the R-value, the more effective the insulation is in keeping a house warm in winter and cool in summer.) Matthew and Clark put soffit and ridge vents in to allow adequate airflow in the attic.

During a six-month period, our electric bill ranged from a high of $18 to a low of $13. The gas and water bills are similarly modest, thanks to these types of small changes throughout the house.

The kids and I planted apple, pear, peach, and cherry trees in our yard and started a vegetable garden on the south side of the house. The garden is prospering, thanks to a load of old manure from a neighbor's farm.

We fit a bicycle with a carrier made from an old milk crate, which makes it safe and convenient for us to run errands without using the car. But the most important energy-saving decision we made was the choice of our home's location. It is two blocks from our children's college, which has eliminated the need to fly them home for school breaks. We also chose a home that allows us to walk to the store, the bank, and work, which means far less time commuting and more time for family and ministry.

In our three decades together, one of the things Matthew and I have learned is that our home is about a whole lot more than Matthew and me. It is about our children, our calling, the example we set, and the legacy we leave.

—*Nancy Sleeth*

Adapted with permission from *Go Green, Save Green: A Simple Guide to Saving Time, Money, and God's Green Earth* (Tyndale, 2009)

Good Steward Action Plan: Man

Instructions

1. Pick two or more new actions from the suggested lists to commit to today, this week, this month, and this year—or come up with your own ways to fulfill the Genesis 2:15 call.
2. Go to blessedearth.org and join our community of Good Stewards. Explore the website to find additional ideas for saving energy and becoming a better steward of God's creation..
3. We will send encouragements to you, and help you stay on track. We're all in this together, so share your journey. Let us know what was easy, and what was difficult; inspire others with your story!

Today, Lord, help me to:

(pick at least two of the following goals, or come up with your own actions)

- Avoid opening the refrigerator door before I know what I want; unplug refrigerators or freezers in the basement or garage that are not in use.
- Avoid using aluminum foil and plastic wrap.
- Turn my hot water heater to a lower setting.
- Learn about the recycling program in my area.
- Drink tap water instead of bottled water, sodas, or sports drinks.
- Read Psalms 23, 24, 104, 147, and 148.
- Ask God to help me become a better steward of His resources.
- Follow our grandmothers' advice: "Use it up, wear it out, make it do, or do without."

1. _____

2. _____

This week, Lord help me to: _____

(pick at least two of the following goals, or come up with your own actions)

- Cut up food into smaller pieces before cooking; put the lid on pans; match the size of the pan to the burner; cook outside in summer.
- Visit the grocery only once each week. Combine trips. Carpool.
- Pre-cycle by avoiding the purchase of items with excessive packaging, individual wrapping, or packaging that cannot be recycled.
- Reduce the amount of junk mail I receive by registering at www.dmaconsumers.org/cgi/offmailinglist.
- Switch to eco-friendly cleaning products, or find recipes for making my own at blessedearth.org.
- Use cloth towels instead of paper; switch to toilet paper and tissues made from recycled paper; avoid using paper plates and paper cups.
- Donate a box of books to the library.
- Find out if my electricity provider offers a green power option and make the switch.
- Wear pants, dresses, sweaters, and skirts several times before washing; iron clothes only when absolutely necessary.

1. _____

2. _____

_____

❝ *The changes we make will not earn our way into heaven, but they do two important things for our souls: they connect us with the family of humanity around the globe, and, more importantly, they bring us closer to God. If He asks us to give up everything we have and follow Him, I now know with certainty that each member of my family would gladly do so. This lack of attachment to things brings us priceless freedom and allows us to hear His call.* **❞**

—*Dr. Matthew Sleeth*

This month, Lord, help me to:

(pick at least two of the following goals, or
come up with your own actions)

- Stock up on handkerchiefs, cloth shopping bags, and cloth napkins; avoid purchasing anything with the word "disposable."
- Air-dry laundry.
- Caulk and weather strip around windows and doors to plug air leaks.
- Avoid covering radiators and vents with furniture or curtains; program thermostats to come on 30 minutes before waking up and coming home.
- Insulate my attic with a minimum of 14 inches of insulation.
- Purchase gently used clothes and gladly accept hand-me-downs.
- Seek out items made from recycled materials.
- Cancel newspaper and magazine subscriptions; instead, share with a friend, read at the library, or catch headlines electronically.
- Wait a month before buying something I "need"; when I do make purchases, buy quality items that will last for many years.
- Clean out clothes closets; give away items I haven't worn in the last year.
- Purchase toys, books, and sports equipment at yard sales.
- Ask my utility company to conduct an energy audit of my house, and make a plan for following up on their advice.

1. _____

2. _____

This year, Lord, help me to:

(pick at least two of the following goals, or come up with your own actions)

- Clean the attic, basement, and garage, and sell or give away items I don't need.
- When replacing appliances, purchase the most efficient (Energy Star), with the lowest yearly energy costs.
- When replacing a car, consider a hybrid or one that gets great mileage and has low emissions.
- Vacation closer to home.
- Insulate my hot water heater and pipes.
- Make or purchase thick or insulated window curtains. Close them during the day in summer; close at night in winter.
- Clean or replace furnace filters every three months.
- Set up a compost bin outside.
- Set up a recycling system for the household.
- Cut back on purchases of makeup, creams, and other personal care products. Look for earth-friendly products when I shop.
- Use ceiling fans instead of the air conditioner.
- Wear layers in winter, put extra blankets on the bed, and use throws to stay warm on the sofa instead of cranking up the heat.
- Go on a spending fast for a week; only buy essentials such as food, gas, and medicines—*nothing* else.

1. _____

2. _____

_____

ℂ *Dear heavenly Father—thank You for the gift of Your creation and the multitude of blessings I take for granted every day. Please fill me with gratitude and a desire to be a better steward of Your gifts. Help me to tend and protect Your garden with a joyful heart.* **🥇**

God created the earth, and it belongs to Him. "The earth is the LORD's and all that is in it, the world, and those who live in it; for he has founded it on the seas, and established it on the rivers." *(Psalm 24:1)*

The first commandment that God gives to humankind is to tend and protect the garden. "The LORD God took the man and put him in the Garden of Eden ..." Why? "... to work it and take care of it." *(Genesis 2:15)*

God entrusted His creation to our care. "We are servants of Christ and stewards of God's mysteries. Moreover, it is required of stewards that they are found trustworthy." *(1 Corinthians 4:1–2)*

A good steward learns to use, but not abuse, God's creation. "If you come on a bird's nest, in any tree or on the ground, with fledglings or eggs, with the mother sitting on the fledglings or on the eggs, you shall not take the mother with the young. Let the mother go, taking only the young for yourself, in order that it may go well with you and you may live long." *(Deuteronomy 22:6–7)*

We will be blessed if we care for God's creation, but cursed if we don't. "But you shall keep my statutes and my ordinances and commit none of these abominations ... otherwise the land will vomit you out for defiling it, as it vomited out the nation that was before you." *(Leviticus 18:26, 28)*

Poor stewardship practices have consequences for humanity and the earth. "Ah, you who join house to house, who add field to field, until there is room for no one but you, and you are left to live alone in the midst of the land! The LORD of hosts has sworn in my hearing: Surely many houses shall be desolate, large and beautiful houses, without inhabitant." *(Isaiah 5:8–10)*

Those who do not care for God's creation will suffer severe penalties. "The nations raged, but your wrath has come, and the time for judging the dead, for rewarding your servants, the prophets and saints and all who fear your name, both small and great, and for destroying those who destroy the earth." *(Revelation 11:18)*

Because God gives us free will, we can choose life or death. God wants us to choose life. "I have set before you life and death, blessings and curses. Choose life so that you and your descendants may live, loving the LORD your God, obeying him, and holding fast to him." *(Deuteronomy 30:19–20)*

Adapted with permission from *The Gospel According to the Earth: Why the Good Book Is a Green Book* by Matthew Sleeth (HarperOne, 2010)

Acknowledgments

This book couldn't have happened without the creative genius of Santino Stoner and David Wenzel. God led us to break bread with you nearly three years ago along the river near Grand Rapids; thank you for your strength and perseverance as we paddled upstream together.

Brett and Corey—we are grateful for your immense talents and your friendship. To the entire Dot&Cross dream team—including Sue, Seth, Michael, and Sally—your belief in our work keeps us going.

We also thank God for our partners at Zondervan—especially John Raymond, Michael Cook, and Sandra Vander Zicht—we are grateful for your willingness to walk with us in faith.

To our partners at HarperOne—including Mickey Maudlin, Emily Grandstaff, and Marlene Baer—thanks for believing in the creation care message and helping us share it with the world.

To our friends and neighbors at Asbury Seminary—including Tom Tumblin, Ginny Proctor, Leslie Andrews, Ellsworth Kallas, and Tim Tennent—it is an honor to reach out to God's Kingdom along side of you.

To Will Sears: you are an answer to prayer. Blessed Earth is indeed blessed by your many talents.

Finally, our loving thanks to the Kendeda Foundation: your generosity, encouragement, and faithful support of Blessed Earth have helped us move mountains.

About Blessed Earth

Blessed Earth is an educational nonprofit that inspires and equips faith communities to become better stewards of the earth. Through outreach to churches, campuses, and media we build bridges that promote measurable environmental change and meaningful spiritual growth.

The Sleeth family's environmental journey has paralleled their faith journey. As they began to live out what it means to love God with all their heart, mind, soul, and strength, and to love their neighbors as themselves, they found their calling: to live more simply. The first and most important miracle for the Sleeths is that their entire family came to know Christ, not just in their heads but in their daily actions. Hanging clothes on the line, washing dishes by hand, and growing their own food are all ways of how they show daily respect for God's creation, and love for their global neighbors.

From these humble beginnings a revolutionary ministry began to grow. Dr. Sleeth wrote a book that received a much wider, more enthusiastic response than he could have ever dreamed. Then, to address larger audiences and respond to the hundreds of speaking requests, the Sleeths formed Blessed Earth. The Sleeths' message has inspired congregations, colleges, and individuals that never had creation care on their radar screen to make huge changes, quickly. When people embrace the principles of simplicity and conservation in their hearts, the difference is dramatic.

Focusing less on material things, and more on relationships with family, friends, and God, leads to happier, more meaningful, and richer lives. With God, all things are possible—including a cleaner, healthier world to leave for future generations.

Additional Resources

Also available from the Sleeths and Blessed Earth:

Blessed Earth: Part 2—Hope for Humanity
Zondervan, 2010.

In *Hope for Humanity*, Dr. Sleeth examines how God's original command to "tend and protect the planet" extends into the actions and activities of our everyday lives. In Sessions 7–12, Dr. Sleeth advocates a spiritually and environmentally sustainable lifestyle, focusing on six elements of life—Rest, Work, Give, Share, Teach, and Hope.

Blessed Earth: Part 2—Hope for Humanity Guidebook
Zondervan, 2010.

Designed for use with the *Hope for Humanity* DVD, this guidebook provides personal questions, practical applications, and additional content to help viewers dig deeper into the creation care lessons of Sessions 7–12. An accompanying Leader's Guide for group discussion is available at blessedearth.org.

Serve God, Save the Planet
Zondervan, 2007.

Dr. J. Matthew Sleeth and his family lived in a big house on the coast, had two luxury cars, and many material possessions. As chief of the medical staff at a large hospital, Sleeth was living the American dream—until he saw an increasing number of his patients suffering from cancer, asthma, and other chronic diseases. Suspecting that the earth and its inhabitants were in trouble, he turned to Jesus for guidance. Dr. Sleeth shares how his family cut their use of resources by more than two-thirds and discovered how the scriptural lessons of personal responsibility, simplicity, and stewardship could lead to a healthier, more joyful life.

Go Green, Save Green
Tyndale House Publishers, 2009.

Many people want to "go green" but put it off because they believe it's too time consuming and too expensive. Not so! Nancy Sleeth and her family have been living an eco-friendly lifestyle for years, saving both time and money. Now, for the first time, she divulges hundreds of practical, easy-to-implement steps that you can take to create substantial money savings while protecting the earth.

It's Easy Being Green
Zondervan/Youth Specialties, 2008.

Want to set your teens on fire for Christ and all of creation? Just fifteen years old when she wrote *It's Easy Being Green*, author/activist Emma Sleeth is a rebel with a cause: saving souls while saving the planet. With real stories from real life, Emma explores how everything we do—from what we eat to how we spend our spare time—impacts the world.

The Gospel According to the Earth
HarperOne, 2010.

In *The Gospel According to the Earth*, Matthew Sleeth retells the often radically countercultural Bible stories that motivated his journey from emergency room doctor to environmental leader, and shows Christians what they can do to care for God's green earth. With passion and faith, Sleeth provides a new green lens through which we can read the Bible to discover answers to our biggest questions of our time and helps us to see afresh how relevant, broad, and deep the Bible's teaching remains.

For more information about the Creation Care journey, visit blessedearth.org,
where you'll find the most comprehensive, interactive Creation Care resources on the web.

Share Your Thoughts

With the Author: Your comments will be forwarded to the author when you send them to *zauthor@zondervan.com.*

With Zondervan: Submit your review of this book by writing to *zreview@zondervan.com.*

Free Online Resources at
www.zondervan.com

Zondervan AuthorTracker: Be notified whenever your favorite authors publish new books, go on tour, or post an update about what's happening in their lives at www.zondervan.com/authortracker.

Daily Bible Verses and Devotions: Enrich your life with daily Bible verses or devotions that help you start every morning focused on God. Visit www.zondervan.com/newsletters.

Free Email Publications: Sign up for newsletters on Christian living, academic resources, church ministry, fiction, children's resources, and more. Visit www.zondervan.com/newsletters.

Zondervan Bible Search: Find and compare Bible passages in a variety of translations at www.zondervanbiblesearch.com.

Other Benefits: Register yourself to receive online benefits like coupons and special offers, or to participate in research.